Oxford Studies of Composers

General Editor : Colin Mason

Egon Wellesz: FUX
Denis Arnold: MARENZIO
Basil Deane: CHERUBINI

FUX

Oxford Studies of Composers (1)

FUX

EGON WELLESZ

London

OXFORD UNIVERSITY PRESS

NEW YORK   TORONTO

1965

Oxford University Press, Amen House, London E.C.4

GLASGOW NEW YORK TORONTO MELBOURNE WELLINGTON
BOMBAY CALCUTTA MADRAS KARACHI LAHORE DACCA
CAPE TOWN SALISBURY NAIROBI IBADAN
KUALA LUMPUR HONG KONG

*Printed in Great Britain
by W. & J. Mackay & Co. Ltd.
Chatham, Kent*

CONTENTS

INTRODUCTION

THE present study is a belated tribute to a composer whom I have admired since I edited his coronation opera *Costanza e Fortezza* half a century ago. The more I studied his music and the documents of his life the more fascinated I became by his dual role as composer and teacher. He was the leading Austrian musician in the first part of the eighteenth century and at the same time an outstanding master of composition, who was adored by his pupils. The devoted servant of three Emperors, honoured on every occasion, he was well aware of his own value. He had a biting wit and could not resist being drawn into endless polemics, when he felt he was in the right.

The importance of the *Gradus ad Parnassum*, unsurpassed as a text-book for the teaching of strict counterpoint, is well known. It served as a model for all later treatises on the subject. Not so well known, however, are the many profound remarks about taste and style in the fragmentary last chapters. One, particularly, seems to reveal his artistic creed: 'A composition meets the demand of good taste if it is well constructed, avoids trivialities as well as wilful eccentricities, aims at the sublime, but moves in a natural way and has the power to please even the experts. . . . An undisciplined composition, even if it embodied some exquisite idea, might tickle the ears of untrained listeners but would never satisfy the fine taste of the connoisseur: brilliant ideas alone will not do, they demand perfect workmanship.'[1]

From such passages as well as from the official reports about the musicians at the Imperial Court we can form a picture of Fux as a teacher of great vitality. He certainly possessed the gift of convincing his pupils that there were many ways, not only one or two, of achieving a satisfactory solution to a problem of composition. He also found generous words of praise and encouragement for musicians who came for advice, when he thought that their work was good.[2] Holzbauer, later famous as the composer of the opera *Günther von Schwarzburg*, wrote that he never came home so happy as when he had visited Fux, who had said to him: 'You are a born genius.'

[1] Fux, *Gradus ad Parnassum* (Vienna, 1725), p. 241.
[2] cf. I. Holzbauer, *Musikalische Correspondenz* (Speyer, 1790), pp. 107 ff.

The picture of Fux as an outmoded theorist[3] who was also a com-poser of church music and court operas is misleading. Had he been such a minor figure, he could not have maintained his prominent position among the brilliant Italian composers who were employed as composers and conductors at the Court in Vienna. His sacred music became part of the repertory. The original vocal parts of his masses in the Vienna Nationalbibliothek bear lists of their first and all subsequent perfor-mances, which show that many of them were performed down to the middle of the century. The *Missa S. Joannis*, composed in 1727, had forty performances, the last given in 1775; the *Missa di San Carlo*, written in 1817, was copied by Michael Haydn in 1757, and was pub-lished twice in the course of the nineteenth century. Though printing of music was rare in the days of Fux, the parts of his *Concentus musico-instrumentalis in septem partes divisus* were published at Nuremberg in 1701, and the festival opera *Elisa* in Amsterdam in 1719. In both cases it was, of course, the Imperial Chest which paid for the printing.

How is it then, we may ask, that Fux is known to us mainly as a theorist? He held the highest positions that a musician could achieve at the Imperial Court, first as Hofcompositor (Court Composer), then as Vice-Hofkapellmeister (Imperial Vice-Conductor) and, from 1715 onwards, as Hofkapellmeister (Imperial Conductor). His name appears in all contemporary dictionaries and theoretical works on music; Forkel, in 1802, gives a list of the composers whom J. S. Bach admired, in which Fux receives first mention, and only after him Handel, Caldara, Kayser, Hasse, Graun and some others.

An answer to the question is not difficult to find. Fux died as Maria Theresa and Frederick II came to the throne. The threat of war forced economy. The days of the splendid 'festa teatrale' were gone. A desire for simplicity and sensibility permeated the arts. A new generation of composers, many of them pupils of Fux, was growing up; they ex-plored the possibilities of the new instrumental forms of symphony and divertimento and of a new kind of opera with simpler harmonies and less counterpoint. There was, moreover, such a galaxy of composers in Vienna in the second half of the eighteenth century that performances of composers of the previous generation were rare, though, as I have already pointed out, some of Fux's liturgical works remained in the repertory of churches in Vienna, Salzburg, Prague, Dresden and the princely monasteries of the Danube.

The revival of interest in Fux began with Ludwig von Köchel's biography, *Johann Josef Fux, Hofcompositor und Hofkapellmeister der*

[3] H. Riemann, *Musiklexikon* (11th edition, 1929), p. 556.

Kaiser Leopold I, Josef I und Karl VI (Vienna 1872). This work is still unsurpassed. It contains a biography and an appreciation of the works, but the larger part of the book consists of a number of appendixes, comprising a list of documents about the appointment of Fux, from the account books of the Imperial household, a list of all the conductors, singers, and instrumentalists of the Imperial Chapel from 1680 to 1740, Fux's testimonials about them from 1715 to 40, and the catalogue of his compositions.

The next step was the publication of some of his music. In 1894 Guido Adler, Professor of the History of Music at Vienna University, founded the *Denkmäler der Tonkunst in Österreich* and opened it with the publication of four masses of Fux. In the course of the years motets, instrumental works, the opera *Costanza e Fortezza*, partitas, keyboard music and solo motets have been published.

It was not until nearly seventy years after the publication of Köchel's biography, however, that a major attempt was made to explore the life and work of Fux in greater detail, when Andreas Liess in 1940 began a series of publications, devoting many years to rousing interest in the works of the Styrian composer, particularly in his native country. His book on Fux[4] gives an excellent appreciation of his work, adds valuable biographical material, and lists a great number of compositions which he discovered, particularly in Prague. It was due to his efforts that the plan of publishing the collected works of Fux at last took shape. Under the editorship of H. Federhofer, Professor at Graz, the J. J. Fux Gesellschaft published five volumes between 1959 and 1963, each of them representing a different genre of composition. The operatic activity of Fux has recently found a most competent interpreter in the Dutch musicologist J. H. van der Meer. His *J. J. Fux als Opernkomponist* (3 vols., Bilthoven, 1961), is a thorough study of the librettos and music of the operas, and of Fux's musical language.

Fux is the first of a long and uninterrupted line of great Austrian composers. When we listen to his music we are suddenly struck by a passage which reveals its origin in the Venetian tradition, others seem to anticipate the classical style of Haydn, but sometimes the warmth and intensity of the melodic line, or the popular character of his minuets remind us of another Austrian musician of peasant stock: Anton Bruckner.

The present study is based on the manuscripts in the Vienna National-Bibliothek, the printed editions of the music and the books and essays mentioned in the bibliography. These are all in German, and

[4] A. Liess, *Johann Joseph Fux* (Vienna, 1948).

Köchel's standard work is very rare. My aim in this volume has been both to introduce Fux to English readers and more generally to put his case again, with music examples that will give some idea of the wide range of forms which he mastered, and will plead more convincingly than words can do for a renascence of his music.

THE LIFE

'BY the grace of God ruling in Heaven we, Mola Mohammed, glorious and almighty Emperor of Babylonia and Judaea, of Orient and Occident, King of all kings . . . we pledge our most sacred word to you Caesar of Rome, and to you King of Poland and to all your subjects that we will invade your little country. With us are thirteen kings and one million three hundred thousand soldiers . . . We order you to attend us in Vienna, your capital, where you shall be beheaded . . . We shall exterminate you and all your subjects . . . but we shall first order them all to be tortured in the cruellest way and afterwards delivered to infamous death . . . You and the King of Poland shall be kept alive until you have seen our pledge fulfilled.'

Thus reads the text of the declaration of war which Sultan Muhammed IV sent to the Emperor Leopold I in 1683. To grasp the gravity of the threat we must understand the political situation. For two centuries the Turks had subjugated more and more of eastern Europe. Hungary, which had flourished under Matthias Corvinus (1458–90), was attacked by the Turks under his successors Ladislas and Louis II. The latter lost his life in the battle of Mohács in 1526. Hungary, as far as the River Tisza, became part of the Turkish realm while Ferdinand of Austria married to Louis's sister claimed possession of western Hungary. Sultan Soliman, however, made a Hungarian nobleman King of Hungary and attacked Vienna in the autumn of 1529, but the garrison repelled all assaults and the Turks had to abandon the siege.

Nevertheless the situation on the eastern frontier remained precarious for more than a century. The Thirty Years War (1618–48) was a constant drain on the resources of Austria, and the Turks renewed their pressure by supporting the revolt of Hungarian Magnates against the Emperor. Finally the Sultan sent against Vienna the vast army which the Manifesto describes. Leopold I and the Court fled to Passau. The fate of Vienna, and of the Empire with it, seemed sealed. For sixty days, however, the garrison under Count Starhemberg repulsed all assaults, until the combined Imperial and Polish Armies under Charles of Lorraine and King John Sobieski of Poland, descending from the mountains north of the city gained an overwhelming victory. The Turks were defeated so heavily that they abandoned their camp with inestimable treasures and fled to Hungary. This was the turning of the tide, the end of the Turkish advance into central Europe. Now the Imperial Army under Prince Eugene of Savoy took the offensive and drove the invaders farther back. His victories at Peterwardein in 1716 and Belgrade in 1717 ended the insecurity which Austria had felt as long as the Turks had occupied Hungary. The years between 1684, when the Court returned to Vienna, and 1740, when the great opponents Maria Theresa and Frederick II of Prussia both came to the throne, were the most prosperous in its history.

Vienna had suffered heavily from the siege in 1683. The town had to be rebuilt, and this occurred when three of the greatest architects of the period were at the disposal of the Court and the nobility to adorn Vienna with the most magnificent churches and palaces. To name only a few of their works, Fischer von Erlach (1656–1723) built the Karlskirche, the Palais Schwarzenberg, and the Winter Palace of Prince Eugene of Savoy; Johann Lucas von Hildebrand (1668–1745) the Belvedere, the summer residence of Prince Eugene; and the great Italian architect and stage designer Galli-Bibbiena built the stages and décors, mainly for Fux's operas, as we shall hear later on. The style of these master builders is known as 'Vienna Baroque'. This was the time when Johann Joseph Fux became the most prominent musician and composer at the Imperial Court; he is the most famous representative in music of the Austrian Baroque.

Fux was born in 1660 at Hirtenfeld in East Styria. His parents were peasants. No document about his years of apprenticeship has been preserved apart from two entries in the registers of the University of Graz, the capital of Styria.[1] The first records his matriculation on 22 May 1680; the second is more explicit: it records that on 22 February 1681 Fux entered the Ferdinandeum, the Jesuit College, which consisted of a public school and the faculties of Theology and Philosophy. The entry reads, 'Joannes Fux, eadem die, Grammatista, Musicus Alumnus Ferdinandei habet lectisternia domus.' This indicates that Fux was accepted as a pupil of the third class, the 'grammatica'[2] of the college, in which Caesar and Cicero were read. He is called 'musicus'. He must therefore already have had some training in theory and singing, a useful preparation for the task which awaited him, since it was

[1] cf. A. Liess, 'Neues aus der biographischen J. J. Fux-Forschung', *Die Musikforschung*, v (1952), pp. 194–200.
[2] The 'Gymnasium' had four classes: (1) Parva, (2) Principia, (3) Grammatica et Syntaxis (Humanitas), (4) Poesis et Rhetorica.

the duty of the alumni to take part in the Service at the Hofkirche (the Church of the Court) at Graz. To the entry of his admission is added in the margin by a later hand: 'profugit clam' (he ran away furtively).

When and in what circumstances did this flight occur? Biographers have rightly wondered how it was possible for the son of poor peasants —who could neither read nor write—to have the opportunity of studying music and of having schooling that enabled him to go to the University. We know from the statutes of the Ferdinandeum that a stipend from the Imperial Treasury was required for alumni entering without private means and that the name of the protector figured on the certificate of admission on whose recommendation the stipend was then granted by the Emperor.[3] On the admission certificate of Fux no protector's name is given. This indicates that the stipend came immediately from the Emperor Leopold I, a passionate lover of music and himself an accomplished and prolific composer. As a boy of 13 Fux may have been presented to Leopold I when the Emperor came to Schloss Eggenburg near Graz, to be married to Claudia Felicitas of Tyrol. The strange fact has also been pointed out that Fux was already 21 years old when he came to the Ferdinandeum to read Caesar and Cicero. That he started so late, though from his early boyhood he had been possessed by the wish to become a musician, was certainly due to his humble origin—one of the points of similarity between him and Bruckner, who was also the son of peasants and brought up in a small village without a proper school. Still more remarkable is the energy with which he must have worked when he did enter the Jesuit College. The Latin in which he wrote his *Gradus ad Parnassum* is remarkably good,[4] and the quotations from classical authors show that he was well read.

We do not know how long he stayed at the Ferdinandeum. Long enough, certainly, to have acquired a good knowledge of the Classics, but too short to finish the academic course. The remark on his flight, 'profugit clam', does not imply anything disreputable in Fux's behaviour, and is explained by a complaint from the Rector in 1692 that members of the Styrian aristocracy encouraged gifted alumni to leave and enter their service as musicians. Fux may have been engaged as organist either at Eggenburg or at the monastery of Seckau, whose Provost was Privy Councillor of Leopold I. In either case strong links would have been formed with the Emperor, which would explain Fux's unprecedented appointment in 1698 as Court Composer by a *motu*

---

[3] ibid., p. 195.
[4] H. Federhofer, 'Beiträge zu G. Muffat und J. J. Fux', *Die Musikforschung*, xiii (1960), pp. 134–42.

proprio of the Emperor, without his having consulted either the Lord High Steward or Antonio Draghi, the Court Conductor, whose duty it was to make recommendations if there was a vacancy in the Imperial Chapel.[5] Reference to the early support of Fux by Leopold I is made in a passage in the dedication of the *Gradus*: 'The work is yours from the beginning, because it was through the support of your illustrious ancestors that my music developed and flourished' (Tuum est origine, quia Inclytorum Antecessorum Tuorum sub Auspiciis Musica mea initium sumpsit et incrementum traxit). These words suggest that Fux had had the support of the Emperor from the beginning of his career, and they confirm the obviously autobiographical passage in the 'Dialogus' with which the second book of the *Gradus ad Parnassum* opens. Here the master Aloysius (that is, Palestrina) asks the pupil Josephus (this is, of course, Fux) if he is aware that the study of music is like an immense sea and that the course of one's life will depend upon the right decision, which must be taken early in life, 'for musicians and poets are born such' (musicus et poeta nascuntur). Josephus answers that he had been most passionately moved by, and drawn towards music, even before he was able to use his intelligence properly; and that now he is filled day and night with sweet sounds even against his will. He could therefore no longer have doubts about his vocation (ità ut de vocationis meae veritate nullam prorsùs dubitandi causam habere mihi videar).

Nothing is known about Fux's career after the entry in the University register of 1681 until his wedding certificate of 5 June 1696 at the Schottenkirche in Vienna, from which we learn that he was well established as organist of that church.[6] The first witness of the signature is Andreas Anton Schmelzer, 'Römisch Kaiserlicher Kammer-Musicus', son of the Court Conductor Heinrich Schmelzer, who had died in 1680. This shows that Fux must have already lived some years in Vienna before he was married, and that he was regarded as a distinguished musician, for the post of organist at the Schottenkirche was the stepping-stone to that at the Imperial Chapel. He must also have been a man of some reputation if Andreas Schmelzer acted as witness to his marriage.

For approximately a decade, from 1683 to 1693, we hear nothing of him. He may have fled to Italy when the Turks invaded Styria in 1683. His instrumental style is certainly influenced by Corelli's technique,[7]

[5] cf. Köchel, *Fux*, pp. 45–46. On the Imperial Chapel see p. 47.
[6] Document reproduced in Köchel, *Fux*, p. 285.
[7] cf. A. Liess, *Fuxiana* (Vienna, 1958), p. 17.

and he may have imbued himself with Palestrina's music, whom he calls in his *Gradus* 'the famous light of music from Praeneste, to whom I owe everything that I know in this art'. His admiration for Italian music lasted his whole life; it found expression in the advice he gave in his old age to the young Holzbauer: 'Go to Italy, and cleanse your head of superfluous ideas.'[8]

The suggestion has also been put forward that Fux spent some years in Prague,[9] and this hypothesis seems at first to be supported by the fact that Liess[10] discovered in Prague forty-eight masses and other liturgical works of Fux which do not appear in Köchel's list. Many of these manuscripts, however, refer to him as 'Maestro di Capella di S. M. Cesarea'; the manuscripts must, therefore, have been brought to Prague, or copied there, after 1715.

Two years after his marriage Fux was appointed Court Composer. This was already a very high post; it could lead to a still higher one, that of Imperial Vice-Conductor, and finally to the highest post which a famous composer could obtain, that of Imperial Conductor. The post of Court Composer should not be thought of as a sinecure; it required hard work, more indeed than might be thought to be within the capacity of one person. He had to write operas and oratorios for all the occasions on which dramatic compositions were performed, particularly the coronation of the Emperor and Empress, their wedding, birthdays and name-days. At carnival time comic operas and masquerades had to be provided, as well as music for receptions at the Imperial residence, at which the Emperor and the Empress, dressed as host and hostess of the 'Black Eagle Inn', used to entertain the nobility. In addition the Court Composer was expected to write masses, graduals, litanies and Te Deums for the Service, suites, serenades and other instrumental music for receptions.

Leopold I had created the post of Court Composer in 1696 for C. A. Badia, but was disappointed that he was interested only in writing operas and oratorios, and these rather sparingly, and not at all in music for the Service. In 1698 the Emperor therefore appointed Fux to the same post, obviously with the instruction to write mainly music for the liturgy and instrumental music.

During the short reign of Joseph I (1705–11) the splendour of the Court increased still further. Joseph was himself a composer and played the flute. The main opera composers at Court at this time were M. Antonio Ziani, Giovanni Bononcini, and Badia. Fux, who by 1702 had written an opera and an oratorio, also now began occasionally to

[8] Köchel, *Fux*, p. 263.   [9] cf. A. Liess, *Fux*, p. 19.   [10] ibid., pp. 61–71.

contribute a one-act dramatic work—a *Poemetto dramatico*, a *Serenata*, or even a *Componimento pastorale-eroico*.

In 1705 Fux was appointed Conductor at the Cathedral of St. Stephan. Here on high feasts the choirs and orchestras of the Imperial Chapel and of St. Stephan's used to combine, particularly when the Court went in procession to the Cathedral. During these years Fux wrote for the Cathedral choir a booklet of elementary exercises, called *Singfundament*, which has come down to us in manuscript.

Shortly before Joseph I died he promoted Ziani to the post of Imperial Conductor and Fux to that of Vice-Conductor, both appointments to date from 1 January 1712. Joseph was succeeded by his brother Charles, King of Spain, who as Emperor had to leave Madrid and take up his residence in Vienna as Charles VI. Like Joseph I, he was a very competent composer, and enjoyed conducting operas from the harpsichord. With his accession to the throne began the period of Fux's greatest activity; in 1715 he was already Imperial Conductor, the highest and most influential post for a musician in the Empire. The appointment made it necessary for him to give up his post at St. Stephan's, and for the following fifteen years he was first and foremost a composer of operas and oratorios.

His dramatic genius, the capacity to encompass a whole scale of contrasting emotions, was fully appreciated by his contemporaries. He reached the height of fame when his festival opera *Costanza e Fortezza*, written in 1723 for the coronation in Prague of Charles VI as King of Bohemia, made him known all over Europe.

In 1731 his wife died and his health was impaired by recurring attacks of gout. He remained head of the Imperial Chapel, but in his last years he was chiefly occupied with administration, most of the conducting being done by Caldara, who died in 1736. On the advice of Fux, Luca Antonio Predieri, Conductor at the Cathedral of Bologna and President of the Philharmonic Society, was called to Vienna in 1738 and became his assistant. Fux retired from office on 30 January 1740, shortly before his death.

In these last years of Fux's life the men who had made Austria a great nation and Vienna a centre of civilization had all died. Prince Eugen, the brother-in-arms of Marlborough, patron of the arts and admirer of Leibniz, whose *Monadologie* he owned in manuscript, died on 21 April 1736; Charles VI on 20 October 1740. At memorial services both for the Prince and for the Emperor the Requiem which Fux had composed in 1697 for the funeral of the Archduchess Eleonora was performed again. Fux died a few months after the Emperor on 13

February 1741. On the day after his funeral the members of the Imperial Chapel performed his mass *In fletu solatium*, from which he had taken the 'Kyrie' and the 'Christe eleison' for his *Gradus ad Parnassum* as models of four- and three-part settings. Fux was, we know, a modest man, but he was supported during his whole life by the appreciation of the Court and of the musicians with whom he worked for more than forty years, and he was well aware of his position in the musical world. Mattheson, a prolific composer and writer on music, had attacked Fux because of the latter's defence of the sol-fa method of teaching singing. When Mattheson asked Fux to send him a biographical note for his *Ehrenpforte*, Fux answered, 'I could write down many favourable facts about my career and the various posts I have held, if it were not incompatible with my idea of modesty to underline my own merits. May it suffice to mention that I have been found worthy of being Charles VI's First Conductor.'

The high esteem in which he was held by his own musicians can be seen from a canon in five parts by the leader of the orchestra of the Imperial Chapel. The words are: 'Inveni hominem secundum cor meum', while two voices sing: 'Joannes Josef Fux, excellens musicus.' Like many great musicians who reach an old age, he was ahead of his time when he began to compose, but was outdated, particularly as an opera composer, by the change in taste which took place between 1730 and 1740. A great number of the Viennese composers who grew up in these years were his pupils. It was not least to his teaching, to his artistic outlook, so dearly observable in all his utterances, and to his rare combination of imagination and mastery of his material, that they owed their ability to introduce into their music a hitherto unknown kind of emotion, and to develop a new form: the Vienna symphony of the seventeen-forties.

THE COMPOSER AND THEORIST

In his thematic catalogue Köchel gives a list of 405 compositions by Fux, most of them large-scale works.[1] To these must now be added those recently discovered by A. Liess, H. Federhofer and others, raising the number to more than 500,[2] an imposing figure, particularly since his activities as head of the Imperial Chapel, as conductor, teacher and theorist must be taken into account. All his composing seems to have been done between 1698, when he was already 38 years old, and 1740, the majority of his work falling between 1708 and 1731, the year of the death of his wife. One is inclined to wonder whether Köchel's dating of the works can be correct. Fux must already have composed some outstanding work when the Emperor, on his own initiative, appointed him Court Composer in 1698. Another fact which makes it seem likely that Fux was at that time known as a composer is the printing of his *Concentus musico-instrumentalis* at Nuremberg in 1701. The printing of music was very expensive, and therefore only works of well-known composers were printed, or those for which a patron paid the costs.

H. Federhofer reminds us, however, that Fux like Bruckner, was late in developing. As we have seen he went to the Jesuit College only when he was 20 years old, and seems to have begun composing when he was a man of 30—though he was then already an accomplished master of his craft.

We cannot separate the composer from the author of the *Gradus ad Parnassum*, the creative artist from the teacher and theorist. The mastery which he taught can be felt in all his compositions. There is, however, a remarkable difference in the application of the rules. In his own compositions he allows himself much more flexibility in the use of hidden octaves and fifths, and particularly in the use of dissonances. This is not surprising: a good teacher will always demand that his pupils observe the rules in the strictest way while they are still learning, in order to give a sound foundation to their technique.

Much has been written about the technique of composition which Fux expounded in the *Gradus ad Parnassum*, but only recently have we gained more information about the origins of his theory and also about

---

[1] Köchel, *Fux*, Beilage X, pp. 1–174.
[2] H. Federhofer, loc. cit., p. 142.

the existence of earlier theoretical writings by Fux. It will be noticed that I speak of a technique of composition and not, as is usual, of a method of counterpoint teaching. Let us first make it clear in Fux's own words that 'counterpoint means composition carried out according to the rules',[3] that the *Gradus* therefore is a treatise of composition in which we not only find a section on fugue but also on accompanied recitative; that he mentions both the 'mixed style' (Choral singing with instruments) and the cappella style ('stylus antiquus') 'which is still in use in many cathedrals and at the Imperial Court in Lent' (*Aula Caesarea tempore quadragesimali*).[4]

It is now known that the *Gradus* was preceded by two other theoretical writings. Under the heading *A Domino J. J. Fux* a number of two-part counterpoint exercises have survived, written after 1700, which differ from those in the *Gradus*. There is also the primer, called *Singfundament*, already mentioned, written for the choristers of St. Stephan's Cathedral, where Fux was conductor and choirmaster until 1715.[5] In working out his system in the *Gradus* Fux was not an innovator. He emphasized, however, that his method was better designed than that of his forerunners to make it easy for the beginners 'to acquire the knowledge of composition step by step, thus enabling them to climb up to the summit of learning as on a ladder'. Fux had a profound knowledge of the treatises on musical theory of the sixteenth and seventeenth centuries. He quotes Zarlino, Giovanni Bononcini, and Angelo Berardi in the chapter about the Modes, but obviously the teaching of composition in Austria must be regarded as the main source for the *Gradus ad Parnassum*. There is a treatise attributed to Alessandro Poglietti (d. 1683) and also to J. K. Kerll. This is identical with the shortened version of the *Tractatus compositionis* by C. Bernhard, a pupil of Heinrich Schütz.[6] Fux therefore transmitted the teaching of Schütz, who had himself taken over that of the great Venetian masters, Giovanni Gabrieli and Monteverdi. It was Schütz indeed who made the division between 'stylus gravis' or 'antiquus', and of 'stylus modernus' or 'luxurians'. As the representatives of the 'stylus antiquus' C. Bernhard mentions above all Palestrina, Josquin, Willaert, Gombert, and the Gabrielis; from their style derived the teaching of strict counterpoint. The 'stylus luxurians' which begins about 1600 does not change the

[3] Fux, *Gradus*, p. 45.
[4] ibid., p. 243.
[5] H. Federhofer, 'J. J. Fux als Musiktheoretiker', *H. Albrecht in memoriam* (Kassel, 1962), p. 109.
[6] cf. H. Federhofer, 'Zur Überlieferung der Musiktheorie in Österreich', *Die Musikforschung*, xi (1958), pp. 164–279.

rules of the 'stylus antiquus', but is, in the words of Bernhard, an elaboration of it 'in which dissonances are used in a certain way which makes them pleasant and shows the skill of the composer'. In dealing more thoroughly with the 'stylus antiquus' than with the new style— which Fux calls 'mixtus' and 'recitativus', but not 'luxurians'—he follows Schütz's advice that nobody can write good music who has not done exercises in the purely vocal style without an accompaniment by a figured bass.[7]

The *Gradus ad Parnassum* was published towards the end of the Baroque period, when composers began to write in a lighter style which on the one hand led to the *style galant*, on the other to the pre-classical style. Mattheson, we know, attacked Fux's method as old-fashioned. Leopold Mizler, however, a pupil of J. S. Bach, translated the *Gradus* into German in 1742, as it were 'under Bach's very eye'[8] and wrote: 'Fux dealt with the fundamental principles of harmony and counterpoint, which always existed, which are still valid and will be valid as long as the system of the world remains unchanged and the rules according to which it exists . . . Though taste may alter, the fundamental principles of composition remain unaltered.'[9] Mizler was right. His German translation was followed by an Italian one in 1761, an English in 1770 and a French in 1773. Haydn and Mozart learned according to the *Gradus*; Haydn even compiled an 'elementary handbook of the various species of counterpoint from the major works of the Conductor Fux'.[10] Moreover, the books on counterpoint by Beethoven's teacher Albrechtsberger, by Cherubini, Bellermann and many others are based on the *Gradus ad Parnassum*, particularly E. Tittel's remarkable *Der neue Gradus, Lehrbuch des strengen Satzes nach J. J. Fux*.[11]

How far, we may ask, does the creative work of Fux reflect the teaching laid down in the *Gradus*? At first there would seem to be a gap between theory and practice, because in the *Gradus* it is mainly the theory of writing in the 'old style' which is expounded. But we must look at the last pages. Here Fux speaks of a capella style with organ and instrumental accompaniment 'which enjoys greater freedom in rhythm, melody and movement'; finally Fux touches on the question of the

[7] H. Schütz, preface to *Musicalia ad chorum* (1648).

[8] P. Spitta, *J. S. Bach*, transl. by C. Bell and J. A. Fuller Maitland, iii (London, 1899), p. 125.

[9] cf. H. Federhofer, 'Der *Gradus ad Parnassum* von J. J. Fux und seine Vorläufer in Österreich', *Musikerziehung*, xi (1957/8), p. 31.

[10] I. Kecskeméti, Introduction to the Te Deum in *J. J. Fux, Sämtliche Werke*, ii, 1 (1963), p. vii.

[11] 2 vols. (Vienna, 1959).

'mixed style' for soloists with chorus and instruments, and deals with 'recitativo accompagnato' in which the music is 'elated speech' (*oratoria elocutio*).

We must remember the musical situation at the time when Fux wrote his *Gradus*. He had grown up in the artistic atmosphere which prevailed in Austria towards the end of the seventeenth century—the period of Viennese Baroque. In music the Baroque style is characterized by 'a careful consideration of the harmonic structure and, in connection with it, the gradual freeing of dissonance; the beginning of an instrumental style utilizing the special qualities of the instruments to enliven the melody as such', predominance of a highest vocal part with coloratura used for sound painting and the use of contrasts between piano and forte, solo and tutti, as in architecture use is made of optical illusion by contrasting light and shadow.[12]

These features characterize the compositions of Fux down to the second decade of the eighteenth century, when obviously a reaction set in. Like Alessandro Scarlatti he now began to admire Palestrina, that brightest light of Music (Clarissimum illud Musicae lumen), and started to model some of his own liturgical compositions on those of his idol. Moreover he took the 'stylus antiquus' as the basis for his own teaching and laid down its principles in the *Gradus ad Parnassum*. But we should not overlook the very important fact that of all the fifty masses for which Köchel gives the scoring, only three—the *Missa Vicissitudinis*, the *Missa Quadragesimalis* and the *Missa Canonica*—are composed in the strict 'stylus antiquus'; to these must be added a few graduals, offertories and hymns. At the height of his fame, experienced in every kind of contemporary music, Fux considered the 'stylus antiquus' an ideal medium for embellishing the liturgy; a style free from human passions, in which the melodic lines given to each voice are blended together in smoothly flowing harmonies. Giving in his *Gradus* as an example of the a cappella style the 'Kyrie eleison' from his *Missa Vicissitudinis*[13] Fux explains that the composer must introduce new turns of the melody and modulations in order to prevent the 'frequent but necessary repetition of the same words, as for example, "Kyrie" and "Amen" causing nausea'.[14] He then gives as an example the development of the 'Kyrie' and asks Josephus, the pupil, if he wants an explanation:

[12] See 'The Beginning of Baroque in Music' in my *Essays on Opera* (London, 1950), pp. 13–32.
[13] *Gradus*, pp. 244–6.
[14] ibid., p. 244.

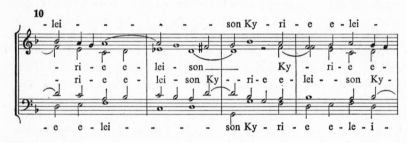

Josephus answers: 'I see and admire the interlocking of the theme in all parts, which are so closely connected that the theme occurs in nearly every bar, here in one, there in two parts, easy and simple to sing, and also with full harmony; so perfect indeed that the theme itself achieves the modulation.' We can understand the admiration of the pupil (or should we say the satisfaction of Fux?) when we analyse the movement of the four parts and notice that in the sixth bar the entry of the soprano on D brings about a modulation from F to C without the insertion of any notes to lead from one key to the other. Fux uses the same canonic technique in the *Missa Quadragesimalis*, but his most famous work in the 'stylus antiquus' is the *Missa di San Carlo*, better known as *Missa Canonica a Capella*.

In his dedication of it to Charles VI he proudly states that he has found it his duty 'to refute for that glorious art the unfounded view of some people, that in the course of time the substance of the old music ("la sostanza della musica antica") has been so much reduced that gradually even its meaning has disappeared and nothing has remained but the shadow of its name which has now been taken over by modern music' . . . 'I flatter myself', Fux continues, 'that your Majesty will see from this Mass that fortunately the old music has not vanished completely.' Fux shows amazing skill in using a different canonic pattern in each section of the Mass, and in spite of the most complicated technical devices he succeeds in producing music which is alive and sounds beautiful.

The four-part 'Kyrie' is built up of two canons. The first is answered 'in nona alta', a ninth higher than the bass, in the alto; the second canon in the soprano is answered 'in nona bassa', a ninth below in the tenor part:

In all the fourteen sections of the mass different canonic devices are employed, so that the Italian sub-title *Tutta in Canone e particolarmente diversificata* is fully justified. One more example will have to suffice, from the opening of the section of the 'Credo' which begins with the words 'Crucifixus etiam pro nobis'. Here two different canonic devices are combined, as can be seen from the explanatory terms set to each of the parts:

Soprano : Resolutio in 4ª alta
Alto : Canone
Tenor : Resolutio in 2ª alta per movimenti contrari
Bass : Canone

This means that the bass begins the canon and the tenor answers with the inversion of the canon a second higher (E–F), whereas in the alto and soprano canon the answer is a fourth above (E–A):

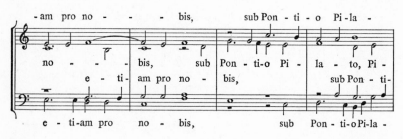

To the masses in the 'stylus antiquus' may be added the offertories *Ad te Domine levavi* of the first Sunday of Advent and *Ave Maria* of the fourth Sunday. Both are presented by Fux in the *Gradus* as models of perfect writing in the 'stylus antiquus'. The rules for this are less strictly observed if to the four- or five-part *a cappella* writing a figured bass for the organ is added. As we shall see, when Fux is writing for chorus and instruments he employs a different technique, the 'stylus mixtus'. In this style, Fux explains, the music enjoys greater freedom in modulating, singing and wandering about (*majori et modulandi et canendi, vagandique gaudet libertate*).[15] From the three examples Fux gives in the *Gradus*, the 'Amen' from the *Missa Credo in unum Deum* may serve as an example:

Here again Fux, in the role of Aloysius, draws his pupil's attention to the use of ligatures. 'Study the modulation which, though not ordinary,

15 *Gradus*, p. 262.

is simple and easy. Look also at the conjunction of the parts on which the power of the harmony rests, and at the motion which continues uninterrupted to the end.'[16] The pupil again expresses his admiration, but asks why it is that the dissonances are resolved in an upward direction against Fux's own advice. The teacher tactfully replies that exactly the same question had been put by an excellent musician, who had not noticed that the note in question was only part of an ornament and inserted for the sake of better melodic movement. The 'substance', the melodic skeleton of the first three bars, was as follows:

Josephus apologizes for not having noticed that the ascending note is part of the melodic decoration, but he has still another question: why are there two F sharps in bar 9, one in the alto, the other in the tenor, a duplication which the master himself has forbidden? Aloysius says that the *diesis*, the sharpening in two parts, is forbidden because the sharpened notes upset the balance of the harmony, but only, of course, if both notes are long. The F sharp in the tenor, however, has very little weight; it is maintained only for the sake of the melodic movement.

I am afraid we would agree here with the arguments of the pupil rather than with those of the master. To our ear the whole sequential chain of eleven bars sounds unsatisfactory; not only are there too many hidden octaves, and in bars 9 to 11 even hidden parallel fifths, but we might also dislike the upward movement of two, and later four, parts without any compensating movement in the opposite direction. But here we must allow that the age in which Fux lived had a different perception of time and space in music from ours, and that Fux, shaping his contrapuntal writing on the model of Palestrina, admitted what we would call parallel fifths and octaves.[17] Their effect was undoubtedly corrected in performance by a clever realization of the figured bass on the organ.

The *Missa Canonica* has always found admirers, even if Fux's fame was not as widespread as that of Palestrina. One always comes back to an art which tends towards the sublime, and one moreover in which

---

16 *Gradus*, p. 271.
17 See A. Liess, *Die Triosonaten von J. J. Fux* (Berlin, 1940), pp. 28–38.

part-writing and harmony are of equal importance. However, we should not exaggerate the importance of the pure a cappella style in the creative output of Fux, but must remember the great variety of musical genres that he employed. It is not yet possible to attempt to date the many works that have come down to us without any indication of the period of his life to which they belong. The difficulty of dating them is increased by the fact that the greater part of the liturgical music survives in parts only, without score. Fortunately, however, the compositions which are available either in handwritten scores or in print are those which were regarded as representative by Fux's contemporaries, and they give us a fairly good idea of his creative activity.

THE WORK

Music for Instruments

FUX marked as his op. I the cycle of seven partitas entitled *Concentus musico-instrumentalis*. This work was dedicated to Emperor Leopold I's son, Joseph, then King of Rome, who had accepted the dedication and had paid for the printing of the parts which were published in Nuremberg in 1701.

The first of the partitas is a serenade for two clarini, two oboes, strings and continuo. It begins with a *Marche*, followed by a *Guique* (prestissimo), a *Minuet* and an *Aria*; then comes an *Ouverture* followed by a *Minuet* with *Trio*, another *Guique* (prestissimo), two *Arias* of different character, two *Bourées*, an *Intrada*, a *Rigadon*, a *Ciacona*, a *Guique*, a *Minuet* and a *Final*.

Ouverture and intrada are used regularly as opening pieces of a suite. We may therefore assume that the serenade consists of three suites. performed on a festive occasion and put together under a single title. I have shown[1] that the ballet suites which were performed at the Court in Vienna between 1665 and 1700 consisted mostly of three to five dances, though sets of six to nine can also be found, particularly in the works of Johann Heinrich Schmelzer, whose son Andreas Anton, as we know, was best man at Fux's wedding.

Of the seven partitas the first, the serenade, is the only one in which two clarini are employed; the second and fourth are scored for two oboes, bassoon, strings, and harpsichord; the third and fifth for strings and harpsichord. The seventh partita is scored for flute, oboe, bass, and harpsichord. Some movements have witty titles, as found in French suites. The Sinfonia (adagio–allegro) is followed by an allegro movement headed 'La joye des fidels sujets'. The third piece combines an Italian aria and a French air. The aria, played on the flute, is in $\frac{6}{8}$, the air (written 'Aire') played on the oboe and the accompanying harpsichord and bass in $\frac{4}{4}$. We may note that in the Italian aria the solo instrument is called 'flauto', in the French air called 'hautbois'. The bold idea of combining melodies of two different measures anticipates by eighty-six

[1] E. Wellesz, 'Die Ballett-Suiten von J. H. und A. A. Schmelzer'. *Sitzungsber. d. Kais. Akademie d. Wiss. Phil. Hist. Klasse*, 176. Bd. 5. Abt. (Wien, 1914).

years Mozart's similar stroke of genius in the ball scene of *Don Giovanni*.

The fourth and last movement has the title 'Les enemis confus'.
These partitas by the young composer were written for the entertainment of the Court on festive occasions, though some movements are in contrapuntal style. The partitas in three parts, as Köchel rightly pointed out,[2] represent a different kind of music. They were 'sonate da chiesa' and had their place in Solemn Mass between epistle and gospel,

[2] *Fux*, p. 57.

where, in fact, they replaced the graduals. All these 'sonate a tre', of which Köchel found thirty-eight in the archives of the Imperial Chapel, show a high artistic standard, as can be seen from the beginning of Partita in G minor (No. 320) reproduced on p. 461 of Köchel:

Fux's mastery in this genre was widely acknowledged. Even Mattheson, who attacked the *Gradus* and was not on good terms with its author, wrote: 'To my humble mind the true mastery of a composer can better be seen from a duo in a good fugal style than from a four-part counterpoint or Allabreve. Thus the trios for instruments have their merits and require a trained man; in that genre the Imperial First Conductor Fux is unsurpassed.'

Recently new light has been shed on the keyboard music of Fux. It consists of sonatas and suites which can be played on the organ as well as on the harpsichord; they may not reach the perfection of the trio sonatas, but they are an important link in the series of Austrian keyboard compositions, beginning with Froberger and leading through Poglietti, F. T. Richter, and G. Reutter to Fux, and from him to his pupil Gottlieb Muffat[3] (1690–1770), the composer of the 'Componimenti Musicali' in 1739. It seems likely that Fux was indebted to Tobias Richter, Court Organist in Vienna, for some of the Austrian features in these compositions, while their French traits go back to François Couperin. A new wave of French cultural penetration had followed the signing of a treaty against the Turks between Austria and France, and it may well be that the partitas for harpsichord were written

[3] G. Adler, *Denkmäler der Tonkunst in Österreich*, iii/3, p. xxi.

at the time of that rapprochement.[4] The first bars of the three movements of the seventh sonata[5] well illustrate the style of these keyboard compositions:

We may note that these pieces, written in D minor, have no B flat signature. Fux treats the D minor as a transposed Aeolian mode, as was the habit still among some of his contemporaries. As a composer, however, he thought and wrote harmonically in the major and minor scales, particularly in his instrumental works and in his operas and oratorios, but also in his liturgical works for mixed choir and orchestra, as will be shown in the following chapter.

Music for the Liturgy

The bulk of the creative work of Fux consists of compositions for the Service, most of them written for performance in the Imperial Chapel, and in St. Stephan's Church, the Cathedral of Vienna.

[4] E. Schenk, ibid., Bd. 85 (1947), p. vii.   [5] ibid., pp. 17 ff.

The first records of payments for the Hofmusikkapelle (this term designates the entire personnel of the Chapel: soloists, chorus and orchestra as well as the conductors) in the accounts of the Office of the Paymaster to the Imperial Court[6] date from 1543. We therefore know the names and salaries of all the musicians from that time down to the end of the Habsburg monarchy. The hey-day of the Hofmusikkapelle was from 1642 to 1740, when, during the reigns of Ferdinand III, Leopold I, Joseph I, and Charles VI, operas, oratorios, and ballets were added to the performances of music for the liturgy and divertimenti for the entertainment of the Court. However, although composing and performing secular music took much of the time of the composer, his main duty was still to write music for the daily Service, for the High Feasts of the Church and for the celebration of important events, particularly birthdays and name-days of the Imperial family. That was what Fux had to do. The number of works written for the church is so great that one wonders how it could all have been written by a man who, from his fifties onwards, suffered severely from gout. In Köchel's thematic catalogue the number of liturgical compositions was already very great; but if we add the newly discovered works in the lists of A. Liess and H. Federhofer we arrive at the amazing total of more than 415 compositions for the church, among them eighty-five complete masses.

The masses in the a cappella style have already been discussed. I shall now deal with those in which instruments are used. From Köchel's researches in the archives of the Imperial Court at Vienna we know that Fux had a large orchestra at his disposal: six organists, twenty-three violinists, one viola da gamba player, four cellists, three double basses, four bassoonists, five oboists, four trombonists, one horn player, sixteen trumpeters, two timpani players.

The texture of the liturgical music (not only the masses) of Fux looks—to use a favourite term of his—'naturaliter'; he wanted his music to be performed as it was written, without all the embellishments, ornaments and variations in which singers and instrumentalists used to try to outdo each other, the singers indeed acting as if they were composers. Today, Fux complains, it is no longer necessary for the composer to write variations: this is done *ad nauseam* by the executants; but he continues, 'if only these *were* variations and did not transform the substance of the music so that the composer has difficulty in discovering

[6] L. v. Köchel, *Die Kaiserliche Hof-Musikkapelle in Wien von 1543 bis 1867* (Vienna, 1869). A. Smijers, 'Die Kaiserliche Hofmusik-kapelle von 1543–1619', *Studien zur Musikwissenschaft*, vi, 139–86; vii, 102–42.

his own melody! *Sed quis contra torrentem?* But who can prevail against a torrent?'[7]

It was the publication of the *Missa SSmae Trinitatis*[8] which first helped to correct the view of Fux as a composer that had prevailed when the only work of his which was known was the *Missa Canonica*. The *Missa SSmae Trinitatis* is set for first and second violins, violas in three parts, three trombones, organ and double choir. Here we have a mass in the 'stylus mixtus', but the instruments are still used mainly to support the voices; the same technique is used in the *Missa Purificationis* in the same volume. The fully developed 'stylus mixtus' which, as Fux says, 'is the one most used today in the churches', can be seen in the *Missa Corporis Christi*.[9] It is entirely different from the a cappella style: the choral sections often have instrumental preludes and postludes, and the sopranos are not always given the top line, which we find in the violins or even in the clarini. The line of the voice parts is more like that in contemporary cantatas than that in masses 'in stylo antiquo'. Fux warns his pupil on the one hand not to confuse this style with that of operas and ballets, as is often done, and on the other not to write dull and sterile music without vitality 'which produces disgust rather than devotion'.[10]

The *Missa Corporis Christi* is printed from the autograph score of Fux[11] and dated February 1713. The title pages give the orchestration ('à 4 Voc. Concert., 2 Trombe, 2 Tromboni, 2 Violini Concert'), the composer's name, and the information that he suffered from gout and was confined to his bed ('Authore Joanne Josepho Fux tunc Podagrâ laborante et lectui affixo').

The mass was obviously composed for an important occasion; it was a *Missa Solennis*, and H. Federhofer may be right in believing that it was written by Fux to thank the Emperor for having given him the post of Vice-Kapellmeister on 26 January of that year. Its jubilant character is accentuated by the brilliant orchestration and by the festive character of the music, which permeates even the 'Kyrie' and 'Agnus'. The structure of the 'Kyrie' is unusual, too, the first part being preceded by a sonatina for clarini, trumpets, trombones, bassoon, cellos, bass, and organ. After 'Christe eleison' another, shorter, sinfonia in the style of a fanfare introduces the second 'Kyrie eleison', which, after three bars of full harmony, turns into a quick fugato. The first sonatina has the

[7] *Gradus*, p. 220.
[8] *Denkmäler der Tonkunst in Österreich*, i, 1.
[9] Edited by H. Federhofer in *J. J. Fux, Sämtliche Werke*, i, 1 (1959).
[10] *Gradus*, p. 273.
[11] Bibliothèque du Conservatoire, Paris, Res. F. 1058.

F.–C

powerful sonority characteristic of Giovanni Gabrieli's 'canzone da sonar', which created a new instrumental style. His successors in Venice had handed on this sonorous orchestration to Antonio Draghi and to Heinrich Schmelzer, the forerunners of Fux:

SONATINA

Looking at the 'Kyrie', however, we realize that Fux is entering on a new path which leads to the pre-classical style:

Solo Soprano

though in his richness of harmony, his use of uncommon chords, and his excursions through remote keys he continues the Venetian tradition, as can be seen from the following passage from the 'Credo'. This movement of the mass is divided into seven sections, of which the fourth, 'Et incarnatus est', is marked 'Adagio'. In this section composers usually employ their most striking harmonies, but here the sequence of chords is indeed remarkable.

Part of the 'Credo' is remarkable also for its orchestration. The soprano line is intensified by one cornetto and the first and second violins, the alto by the alto trombone and the violas, the tenor by the tenor trombone, the bass by a bassoon, cellos, and violone. All the parts were also supported by the organ, which performed the figured bass. The cornetto is not mentioned on the title-page, though it is used throughout the mass between the clarini and the alto trombone, acting as it were as a second soprano instrument. It was played by Leopold Pramayer, who must have been a remarkable virtuoso, because he was already 58 years old when he joined the Imperial Chapel in 1712, and held the post until his death at the age of 83.

Fux composed six settings of the Te Deum, only one of which, finished on 2 December 1706, has come down to us in full score, in his own handwriting. The manuscript belonged to Joseph Haydn and was

bought, together with other manuscripts, from his heirs by Prince Nicolas Esterhazy.[12] This work was composed when Fux was Conductor of the Music at St. Stephan's, and it seems to have been written to celebrate either the enthronement of Bishop Franz Ferdinand in the middle of December 1706 or the wedding of Charles III, King of Spain (later the Emperor Charles VI) and Princess Elizabeth Christina.[13]

The Te Deum is scored for solo singers, two choirs, and two orchestras, each consisting of two clarini, timpani, first and second violins, cornetto in unison with the sopranos, alto and tenor trombones with

[12] See I. Kechskeméti, Introduction to the Te Deum, *J. J. Fux Sämtliche Werke*, ii, 1 (1963), p. vii.
[13] ibid., pp. vii, viii.

the altos and tenors, bassoon, violoncellos, violone, and organ. The
first part opens with a festive Allegro, with alternating flourishes of the
trumpets, until in the eighth bar the first choir introduces the main
theme 'Te Deum laudamus', followed by the second choir. The flourish
of the trumpets sounds again and the second choir begins the hymn.
These twelve bars are in brilliant C major, and so are the following four
bars. Then suddenly, by using the sub-mediant A minor, Fux turns to
E major, and then even farther to its dominant chord B major, making
a cadence on E major. Without any intermediary chord Fux then
repeats the twelve C major bars.

The next phrase, 'Te aeternum Patrem', begins with soprano, alto,
and tenor solos on the first inversion of E major, ending on the half
close of C major, and is continued with fanfares on the clarini without

any other accompaniment, the fanfares alternating with the singing of the two choirs and ending with 'Eco carbina', which, according to the editor, means a scarcely audible echo.

The verse 'Tu ad dexteram Dei' is introduced by a ritornello with clarini and full orchestra; the four-part counterpoint of the basses is accompanied only by the two organs. Towards the end the writing is again chordal and the ritornello is set for all the brass:

Attention must be drawn to the short recitativo accompagnato 'Dignare, Domine', assigned to the solo soprano of the first choir. This is followed by the final chorus 'In te Domine, speravi', in which the contrasting thoughts 'speravi' and 'non confundar' form two contrasting musical ideas which are contrapuntally combined from the very first bars. In its rich contrapuntal texture the Te Deum is truly representative of Austrian Baroque music, but its harmonic technique strikes us as somewhat advanced for the period; each section of the hymn is clearly designed in either a major or minor key, and the function of dominant, subdominant, mediant and submediant is already fully developed.

Apart from this Te Deum, Köchel lists another (K.271), composed in 1704 for five-part chorus, which was performed again in 1716 when a son was born to Charles VI. A third one was performed on 5 September 1723 during the coronation festivities in Prague.

The same rich instrumental texture can be observed in the solo motets and antiphons, now available in the new edition of the Collected Works.[14] Fux was near his fiftieth year when he and Caldara began to introduce in Vienna the genre of church music that was already flourishing in Naples. The motets and antiphons are as it were 'sacred cantatas' for chorus with one or two solo da capo arias, introduced by a recitative.

[14] J. J. Fux, Sämtliche Werke, iii, 1, ed. H. and R. Federhofer (1961).

Some of them are so emotional in their expression that they might well have been written for an oratorio or even an opera, as can be seen in the two examples from the antiphon *Alma Redemptoris Mater*[15] for solo soprano, alto trombone, violins, cello, bassoon, violone, and organ. The antiphon opens with a sonatina (Andante), followed by an Allegro in which the trombone is given a virtuoso part:

a) Allegro

The last aria, 'Virgo prius', begins Un poco allegro, with the trombone alternating with the voice. This is a conventional piece which was to display the virtuosity of the voice and the trombone. In the final section, however, beginning with 'peccatorum miserere', the trombone alternates with the soprano in an expressive melody:

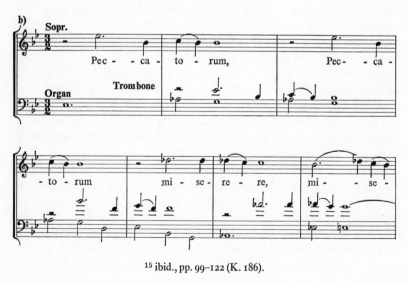

b)

---

[15] ibid., pp. 99–122 (K. 186).

The treatment of the trombone shows how high was the standard of playing in the Imperial Chapel. The trombonist was obviously Leopold Christian. In a petition to have his salary raised Fux claims that 'he is the greatest virtuoso in the world' and that 'there is nobody to equal him'.[16] The high standard continued under his son,[17] and we can easily see that it was this great tradition in the Imperial Chapel which inspired Mozart to write the famous solo in the 'Tuba mirum' of his Requiem.

It has already been pointed out how wide is the gap which separates the *Missa canonica* from the motets and antiphons with their recitatives and arias in the fashionable Neapolitan style, with its intensfied dramatic element. It must now be shown how strongly this element comes into its own in its proper domain in opera and oratorio.

Opera and Oratorio

Opera in Vienna was more than a 'divertissement', a mere entertainment for the Court. The performance of an opera was considered an artistic event of great importance. This was largely due to the fact that from Ferdinand III's accession to the throne in 1637 to the death of Charles VI in 1740, not only were the Emperors interested in contemporary music, they were also competent composers, particularly occupied with opera and oratorio in the Venetian style. It is for this reason that the scores of such works as Monteverdi's *Il Ritorno d'Ulisse* (1641) and Cavalli's *Egisto* have been preserved in the Court archives. However, opera did not gain a footing in Vienna as a regular institution until after the end of the Thirty Years War, and it is not without significance that the first opera to be performed was the 'Drama musicum' by the Emperor Ferdinand III, in 1649. It bore the dedication: 'Ad Athanasium Kircherum ab Imperatore Ferdinando transmissum.' An oratorio was performed in the Imperial Chapel[18] in the same year, but

[16] Köchel, *Fux*, appendix vi, 18, 102.
[17] ibid., appendix vi, 55.
[18] A. v. Weilen, *Zur Wiener Theatergeschichte* (Vienna, 1901), p. 6.

regular performances of oratorios began on Good Friday 1660 with *Il sacrificio d'Abramo* by the Emperor Leopold I.[19]

Apart from the grand oratorio a specific genre for chamber orchestra developed. This kind of 'Rappresentazione Sacra' was called 'Sepolcro', because the action concerned the Crucifixion. Performances took place on Maundy Thursday or Good Friday in the chapel of Eleonora, the widow of the Emperor Ferdinand, and a tomb and the cross were placed in front of the altar. The 'Sepolcro' consisted of an overture, recitatives, and arias; and the genre, of which Antonio Draghi was the unparalleled master, flourished particularly under him in Vienna. To give an example of the high quality of its music, the 'Suonata à 5' of *Il Terremoto* (1682) may be given; it is for violin, soprano, alto, tenor, and bass violas, and figured bass. The piece shows the rich flow of carefully chosen harmonies, which had been a feature of the masters of the Venetian school. The sequence of harmonies, expressing the feelings of the mourners at the cross, is dramatically most effective and moving:

[19] cf. G. Adler, *Musikalische Werke der Kaiser*, ii, nos. 2–4.

By the beginning of the eighteenth century, however, the oratorio had become structurally almost identical with opera seria. Their main difference was that an opera seria was usually in three acts, an oratorio in only two. (In the interval, the duration of which was laid down as not more than a quarter of an hour, one of the Court preachers had to deliver a sermon.) Its content differed widely from that of the early seventeenth-century oratorio which had been intended for devotion. By the time of Fux it had absorbed all the features of the Neapolitan opera, and was, in fact, a coloratura opera based on a text from the Bible.

Fux wrote nineteen operas and ten oratorios between 1700 and 1731. The music of the first operas is lost. The first full score which has come down to us is that of *Julo Ascanio, rè d'Alba*, performed on 17 March 1708.[20] The libretto is by Pier Antonio Bernardoni (1672–1714), who was Court Poet in Vienna from 1703 to 1713. *Julo Ascanio* has been published in Fux's Collected Works.[21] The libretto is based on the

[20] cf. J. H. Van der Meer, *J. J. Fux als Opernkomponist*, i (1961), pp. 63–72.
[21] Serie v, B. 1 (1962).

story of Ascanius, founder of Alba, as told by Livy, and that of Euander in Ovid's *Fasti*. Ascanius has conquered the Teucri and founded Alba. He falls in love with Emilia, the sister of the conquered King. Their marriage brings peace and reconciliation.

The overture, as Van der Meer points out,[22] is a mixture of a French ouverture and an Italian sinfonia; the first, second, and fourth movements have fugato openings, the third movement is an adagio. Some of the arias make use of solo instruments. The first aria achieves a war-like character by the use of a recurring trumpet fanfare; the second, sung by Ascanio, 'Vestito da pietà, Amor nel sen m'entrò', is accompanied by two viole da gamba; the bass aria of Euandro, 'Credo appeno al mio destino' (p. 71), has a rich cello part, and the aria of Carmenta, 'Qual giglio' (p. 158), is set for cembalo and viola da gamba. The most interesting orchestration is that of Emilia's aria, 'T'aborrisco' (p. 111), in which she wavers between hate and love for Ascanio. Her hatred is expressed in the quick, rolling figures on two bassoons, her love in slow chords on the strings:

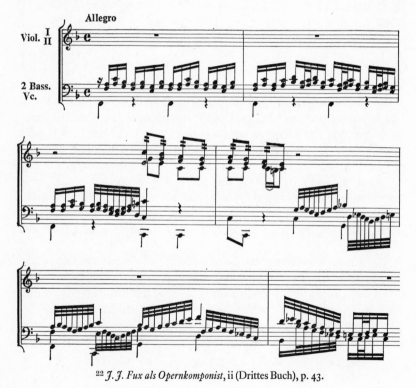

[22] *J. J. Fux als Opernkomponist*, ii (Drittes Buch), p. 43.

The following aria of Ascanio (p. 120), in which he confesses his love to Emilia, is the peak of the opera. In the nineteen bars of the introductory ritornello Fux develops a melody of great warmth and beauty, played on solo violin and accompanied by the harpsichord. The way in which he keeps the melody flowing in always new turns is the work of a master. Only in bars 4-7 can the trace of a sequence be observed, otherwise each bar has its own melodic and rhythmic pattern:

In the following year, 1709, Fux wrote two short name-day operas
of the kind called 'Componimento per musica'. The first, *Gli Ossequi
della Notte*, is written for the name-day of the Empress. Night invites
Architecture, Urania, the Grace Pasitea, Sleep, and Silence to do hom-
age to the Empress. Sleep and Silence first object to being disturbed,
but when they learn the reason they join in the hymns of praise. The
overture makes use of two orchestras with four trumpets, but otherwise
Fux makes use of delicate orchestral effects; thus a sonatina is set for a
chalumeau and a group of solo strings:

One aria is set for viola d'amore and two viole da gamba, another for four viole da gamba in unison.

In the second Componimento, *Il mese di Marte*, the name-day of the Emperor is celebrated. The sinfonia opens with a presto movement in $\frac{6}{8}$ in a gay mood:

The simple, idyllic plot is only a pretext for the prophecy that a glorious monarch will one day have his name-day in March, and for a chorus in praise of Joseph I. In a similar festive mood is *La Decima fatica d'Ercole* of 1710. It is called 'Componimento pastorale-eroico', because the dramatis personae include shepherds on the one hand and Hercules and the Prince of Ister on the other. The music is therefore partly pastoral, partly contrapuntal and martial.

There are no dramatic works after this until 1714, when Fux wrote the oratorio *La fede sacrilega nella morte del Precursor S. Giovanni Battista*, which opens a fertile phase in his dramatic production. From then until 1720 he wrote an opera and an oratorio every year except for 1718, when he produced an oratorio, *Christo nel orto*, but no opera.

The libretto of *La fede sacrilega nella morte del Precursor S. Giovanni Battista* is by Pietro Pariati, who wrote most of the librettos for Fux's operas and oratorios. Pariati was born in Reggio-Emilia, studied law and took the degree of Doctor juris in 1687. He fell into disgrace with his sovereign, the Duke Rinaldo of Modena, obviously for political reasons, was imprisoned, and afterwards had to leave his country. He then settled in Venice, where he began to write plays and librettos which aroused the interest of Apostolo Zeno, who had already established his fame as a librettist. Pariati's renown as a dramatic writer quickly grew. Charles VI called him to Vienna in 1713 as Court Poet, and he remained in that post until his death in 1733. Apostolo Zeno was appointed to the same post in 1718, and both collaborated in the dramatic reform which received final shape in Metastasio's librettos. Zeno favoured historical themes, whereas Pariati based his plots mostly on mythological subjects which he treated with great freedom. Here love is the dominant force, as it was to be in the plays of Metastasio.[23] Pariati is a true Court Poet; his heroes are idealized representatives of the reigning monarchs. His fame has been overshadowed by that of Zeno and Metastasio, yet turning again to *La fede sacrilega* one finds that the plot is well constructed and offers Fux a perfect opportunity to write dramatic music.

The oratorio opens with a sinfonia in the French style, i.e. Andante-Allegro assai. After five bars of the andante in crotchets the strings play the following passage, which clearly develops a mood similar to that which we saw in the suonata from Draghi's *Il Terremoto*. We have here chords of a boldness like that of the 'Sepolcro' of 1682 (Ex. 18), but the melodic line rises and descends with inexorable logic:

[23] cf. N. Campanini, *Un precursore del Metastasio* (Biblioteca critica della Letteratura Italiana) (Florence, 1904).

The tragic mood of the slow movement is instantly dropped in the Allegro assai. The agitated passages of the violins, the energetic fugato sections of this movement are an apt preparation for the festive atmosphere of the first scenes, in which Herod's birthday is celebrated. The chorus of the people is a Siciliano in two stanzas, pastoral in character. Herod expresses his happiness at the good wishes of his people, but he sees that his daughter Oletria[24] is sad. She reveals that she and her mother have been humiliated by a religious fanatic, and in a passionate aria she demands vengeance. Herod promises to punish the traitor. Suddenly St. John stands in their midst and says: 'I am the traitor.' He denounces Herodias for turning against him, she is the one who is guilty; but the voice of God cannot be silenced. Herod warns him not to go too far in his accusations, and promises to forgive him. But now Herodias appears and in a most effective slow aria implores Herod to avenge her. St. John entreats Herod to give Herodias back to his own brother, whose wife she was, but Oletria, remonstrating with Herod, expresses in an aria her idea of royalty:

> Non è sempre la clemenza
> Gran virtù di un Regio core

(Mildness is not always the supreme virtue of a king's heart.) Herod

[24] Salome is here called Oletria, the Greek name for 'the pernicious one'. cf. L. Ergens in the 'Literarhistorische Einleitung' to *Fux, Sämtliche Werke*, iv, 1 'Oratorien', p. xvii.

tries to avoid persecuting the prophet, and is torn by the conflicting forces in his breast (Nature condemns me, my heart absolves me) and reveals his despair. Then Herodias and Oletria both attack St. John. A brilliant terzetto follows in which they threaten him with death, and St. John declares his readiness to gain the palm of martyrdom. A madrigal ends the first part in which the chorus sings that 'Innocence, faith and pity follow the Precursor'.

In the second part the conflict is carried farther. The arias of Herodias and Oletria would be repetitious if Fux's dramatic genius had not given each aria a new emotional character, as when Herodias, in a seemingly tender song, says that she does not speak out of hatred of the prophet, but of fear for her beloved. A message that the people are suddenly in uproar leads to the crisis. St. John is accused of high treason. He defends himself in an expressive recitative: how could he, one single man, cause the revolt? But he must speak out what is the truth: 'Stella di verità precorro, e sieguo de la giustizia il sole' (I walk in advance, star of truth, and follow the sun of justice). Finally Herod is forced to imprison the prophet, and invites his retinue to a feast. He asks Oletria to dance for him, and Oletria dances to the sound of a gay chorus. Herod, in ecstasy, asks her to demand whatever she wishes:

Per la fede regal, per la mia vita,
per la gloria di Cesare e di Roma,
per il Ciel, per gli Dei cosi m'impegno,
quando ancor tu pretenda ch'io divida
con te lo scettro e'l regno.

(By my royal oath, by my life, by the glory of Caesar and of Rome, by the heaven, by the gods I so me bind, even if you demand that I should share my sceptre and reign with you.)

Oletria answers:

This ecstatic promise of Herod's reminds us of the similar scene in Oscar Wilde's play. And just like Salome in Richard Strauss's opera, Oletria calmly demands the head of the prophet and continues in a dance-like rhythm to taunt Herod, saying that a king who does not keep his word is not worthy to reign:

At last Herod orders the beheading of the prophet and a soldier rushes off to fulfil Herodias's wish. At this point Fux inserts an aria by Herodias accompanied by a theorbo; in fact, it is a brilliant solo concerto for the theorbo to which the voice adds explanatory words. From the dramatic point of view the aria is intended to fill the gap between the departure of the King's messenger and the last scene, in which he announces the death sentence to the prophet. At first glance the aria with its unusually long ritornellos seems out of place in an oratorio. We must remember, however, that it was quite usual in operas given between 1660 and 1730 for the Emperors to insert arias of their own composition. Here Fux may have been asked to insert a theorbo concerto for his colleague, Francesco Conti, who was considered the greatest virtuoso on the instrument in the whole world[25] and had been made Court Composer shortly before. The triumphant aria is followed by Herod's recitativo accompagnato, in which he regrets the fatal oath

[25] Köchel, *Fux*, pp. 94–95, 226.

which brought about all the evil and misery. The last scene is given to St. John, who prays to God for the sinner and is prepared to receive the crown of martyrdom. In a final chorus the moral of the oratorio is given: It is truly virtuous to glorify God in face of tyranny and death.

Pariati's oratorio may, in fact, reflect his own feelings of bitterness at having suffered imprisonment and exile when he had become involved in defending the cause which he considered right. His personal experiences certainly intensified his dramatic poem, and for the music we must agree with H. Zelzer, the editor of the oratorio, that this early work already showed Fux's great talent as a dramatic composer.

Two years later Fux wrote his first large-scale work for the stage: *Angelica vincitrice di Alcina*, a 'festa teatrale' in three acts. It was performed on the huge fish pond in the park of the Imperial Palace called 'Favorita', on 13, 14, 20 and 21 September 1716. The libretto by Pariati was based on Ariosto's *Orlando furioso*, but the plot was handled with great poetic licence. The décor was of unusual splendour. The scenes were built on two islands of the pond by Giuseppe Galli-Bibbiena, mentioned already as one of the most famous architects of that period. He was the son of Ferdinando Galli-Bibbiena, whose main work had been the construction of elaborate stage designs. His son perfected the illusionist technique which aimed at dissolving the walls by paintings which seemed to open a vista on to infinite space. The eye of the spectator nowhere rests on the straight lines of architectural forms, but on reflections of light and shade—an impression which was intensified by the colourful orchestration and the coloratura of the singers. Lady Mary Wortley Montague saw the opera during her stay in Vienna in September and October 1716, and wrote in a letter of 14 September to Alexander Pope: . . . 'Nothing of that kind ever was more magnificent; and I can easily believe, what I was told, that the decorations and habits cost the emperor thirty thousand pound sterling. The stage was built over a very large canal, and, at the beginning of the second act, divided into two parts, discovering the water, on which there immediately came from different parts two fleets of little gilded vessels, that gave the representation of a naval fight. It is not easy to imagine the beauty of this scene, which I took particular notice of: but all the rest were perfectly fine in their kind. The story of the opera was the enchantment of Alcina, which gives opportunities for great variety of machines and changes of the scenes, which are performed with a surprising swiftness. The theatre is so large that 'tis hard to carry the eye to the end of it; and the habits, in the utmost magnificence, to the number of one hundred and eight. No house could hold such large decorations; but the ladies all sitting in the open air, exposes them to great inconveniences; for there is but one canopy for the imperial family; and, the first night it was represented, a heavy shower of rain happening, the opera was broke off, and the company crowded away in such confusion, that I was almost squeezed to death.'

The orchestra of *Angelica* has a large brass section, since the opera was performed in a garden; there are ensembles in which eight trumpets and two pairs of timpani are added to the usual body of strings, reinforced by oboes and bassoons. A high point of the opera is the recitativo accompagnato of Alcina, in which she conjures up Megera, the furies, spirits, and shadows, and orders them to fill the happy islands with monsters:

It may be noticed that Fux follows the dramatic convention of his time in setting the culminating scenes of his operas as recitativo accompagnato.[26] The scene begins in D minor, in the seventh bar reaches F sharp major as dominant of B major, goes back to A major, D minor, F major, B flat major, E flat major, and ends in B flat major. This recitative is full of unexpected intervals for the voice; it is indeed, as Van der Meer observes, one of the most passionate and violent pieces of music that Fux wrote—not surprisingly, since the text of Pariati's scene is based on Seneca's Megara scene in his *Hercules furiens*. Side

[26] cf. my preface to *Costanza e Fortezza* (*Denkmäler der Tonkunst in Österreich*, xvii, 1910) p. xxii, where the beginning of Alcina's conjuration is also given. Van der Meer gives the accompagnato in Ex. 54 of his *J. J. Fux als Opernkomponist*.

by side with this scene, however, with the ferocious dance of the furies, and other scenes of an almost romantic character, we find in the second act a minuet which looks forward to Haydn:

The only opera of Fux which was printed in his lifetime was *Elisa*, a 'festa teatrale per musica'. The libretto was again by Pariati and the performance took place on 25 August 1719 to celebrate the birthday of the Empress, which occurred three days later. The Vienna National-bibliothek posseses a luxuriously bound copy of the score which was published by Jeanne Roger in Amsterdam, obviously the one from which Charles VI once conducted the opera and which he presented to the Empress.

The opera seems to have been so successful that it was repeated ten years later, on 31 August 1729. The action is taken from the episode in Virgil's *Aeneid* where Aeneas and Elisa (Dido) are surprised by a storm while they are hunting. Unlike his source, Pariati builds up a series of love intrigues in which there are many outbursts of jealousy. But finally Aeneas and Elisa are united again with the help of Venus, Amor and Hymenaeus.

The opera was given in the park of the 'Favorita' Palace, and since it was an open-air performance the scoring was for two orchestras each of which had two clarini, two trumpets, timpani, oboes, and strings. There were also two groups for the hunting chorus, each of two horns, strings with woodwind doubling, and figured bass instruments. The horn fanfares which introduce the chorus are remarkable. Indeed, hearing these horns and the chorus of the hunters we seem to be listening to a Romantic opera:

In 1723 Fux was again commissioned to celebrate the Empress's birthday, but this time her birthday coincided with the festivities in Prague arranged for the coronation of Charles VI and the Empress as King and Queen of Bohemia. The opera therefore had to have an action which would symbolize the glory of the monarchy, and Pariati chose one to which he could give as title the device of Charles VI: 'Constantia et Fortitudine.' It had also to demonstrate the magnificence of the Empire in order to gain the support of the powerful Bohemian aristocracy when Charles invoked the so-called Pragmatic Sanction, by which his daughter, Maria Theresa, was enabled to succeed him.

For the first time since the disaster caused by the Thirty Years War, the Court was to go to Prague. From 1700 onwards the city had begun to flourish again, and some of the leading aristocratic families returned and had palaces built by famous architects, including even Fischer von Erlach, the greatest of the Austrian architects, who was commissioned to build the Clam-Gallas Palace.

For the performance of *Costanza e Fortezza* Galli-Bibbiena had to build an open-air theatre on the Hradshin next to the Royal Palace, with an auditorium for four thousand spectators. The magnificence of the theatre and the scenes can be seen from the engravings which were added to the printed libretto.[27] The *Wiener Diarium* reports for 28 August, the birthday of the Empress, 'everybody appeared in full Court dress at the Royal Palace to offer the usual compliments. Towards eleven o'clock all went to Mass at Saint Thomas's and afterwards back to the Palace, where dinner was served. In the afternoon the Emperor, the Empress and all their guests went to hear the opera.'

[27] See my edition of *Costanza e Fortezza* (*Denkmäler der Tonkunst in Österreich*).

46

The prospectus of the stage and the auditorium shows the Emperor and the Empress sitting under a canopy, the foreign princes and guests on both sides of the theatre, while the centre of the auditorium was occupied by the retinue, who had to stand. We can well understand Apostolo Zeno's letter to his brother in Venice, in which he talks of the ever-increasing number of princes and noblemen coming day after day to Prague for the birthday of Elizabeth Christina. Speaking of the opera, he says that it cost the Emperor more than 50,000 florins, 'The place can hold four thousand people, but I won't be one of them, because I do not wish to suffer more than six hours' inconvenience in the open air and especially at night only for the pleasure of hearing it. It would be the same, if it were my own work.'[28]

The most vivid and detailed account of the performance comes from J. J. Quantz, who travelled to Prague to hear the opera with C. H. Graun, the composer, and Weiss, a famous lutenist from Dresden. It was published by Marpurg in his collection of autobiographies of famous musicians.[29] From there Dr. Burney took it over,[30] but not very accurately: from his description one gets the impression that Fux wrote 'coarse' church music, which lacked character, whereas Quantz pointed out that the music 'which *on paper* may in some places have looked stiff and dry' sounded 'very well in the open, much better even than melodies with many quick notes would have done'.

Fux, at the height of his career, knew perfectly well from long experience that music performed in a vast space, with a hundred singers and two hundred instruments, had to be written in a monumental style and scored likewise, so that Quantz's reference to church music was not out of place. Burney, however, clearly misrepresented Quantz by omitting the essential words that though perhaps the music 'looked stiff and dry *on paper*' it was, in fact, the right kind of music for the occasion, and very effective.

Quantz praises the cast and says that 'there was not an indifferent singer among the principal performers; all were first class'. Charles VI's device 'Constantia et Fortitudine' gave Pariati occasion to choose examples of Roman constancy and fortitude, and he took the story of Porsenna, who, with his Etruscan army, is about to conquer Rome and to re-install the exiled King Tarquinius. But the defence of the bridge over the Tiber by Horatius Cocles, Mucius Scaevola's burning of his

[28] A. Zeno, *Lettere*, 6 vols. (Venice, 1785). Letter of 10 August 1723.
[29] F. W. Marpurg, *Historisch-Kritische Beiträge* (1754–62), i, p. 210.
[30] Dr. Burney, *The present state of music in Germany, the Netherlands and United Provinces* (London, 1773), ii, pp. 177 ff.

own hand, and other valiant deeds induce Porsenna to acknowledge the Roman superiority, and a final chorus sings that the supreme heroes are 'Costanza e Fortezza'.

In the festive scenes Fux employs the same orchestral style as in *Angelica* (1716) and *Elisa* (1719), above all in the introductory sinfonia, where four trumpets in the high and four in the middle register are used. In the first and third movement of the sinfonia the trumpets and timpani are divided into two groups. This antiphonal style goes back, as already mentioned, to the great Venetians; it derived from the two niches for the choirs and their organs in San Marco. Indeed, at first hearing the fanfares of the first movement remind us of those in Monteverdi's Vespers, but the string section in bars 4–6 produces a stronger contrast than any we find in a work of the Old Venetian school. This string section leads to G major; but in bar 7 Fux brings the piece back to C major by abruptly turning the tonic G into the dominant of C major, an effect which we find again some hundred and fifty years later in the first movement of Bruckner's Romantic Symphony:

Indeed, there is nothing stiff or old-fashioned in the score, and there is no indication from the music that Fux was getting old. The choruses are of great variety of mood and rhythm, the arias full of dramatic life and the lyrical ones of startling beauty and melodic richness. The phrases are extended and full of unexpected turns. In the first act there is the aria of Valeria, the daughter of the Consul Valerius. She is a prisoner of the Etruscans, but is brought back to Rome to deliver a peace offer which is rejected by her father. She returns to say farewell to her betrothed, Mucius Scaevola. She assures him that she is his and will never cease to love him. He must always bear in mind that he was and ever will be the fulfilment of her life, her heart of hearts. The aria is set for oboes and bassoons, doubling the strings in the preludes and interludes, but Valeria's singing is accompanied, 'piano,' only by two violins and viola:

Spir-to de la mia Vi - - ta, e co - re del mio

cor, e co - re del mio cor.

It is written in the usual form of a Siciliano; but what an outburst of passion there is in the fourth and fifth bar of her melody, and again in the violins in bar 10, before the repetition of 'e core del mio cor', with the unexpected chord of D major.

These examples must suffice. It is only possible to mention in passing the passionate duet between Mucius and Valeria and the moving lament of Erminia, both high points of the opera, and the choruses, which are part of the dramatic action and show Fux's supreme mastery of this genre.

Costanza e Fortezza, the coronation opera, was also the crowning event of Fux's career. He was at the height of his fame, but the day of his greatest triumph found him unable to conduct his work, because of the gout from which he had suffered for some time. He had to be carried in a sedan to Prague and was given a place of honour at the performance near the Imperial canopy. The conductor was Antonio Caldara, who, from now on, acted more and more for Fux.

Fux was 63 years old when this opera was performed. We can well imagine that he felt that he had written his *chef d'oeuvre* and should not try to follow it immediately by a work which might be less inspired. In the following year he seems to have devoted all his time and energy to writing the *Gradus ad Parnassum*, which was published in 1725. In the same year a one-act 'festa teatrale', *Giunone Placata*, was performed on the name-day of Elisabeth Christina, Monday, 19 November. It was written for a small orchestra and was rather a 'componimento di musica'[31] than a festive grand opera.

[31] cf. Van der Meer, op. cit., i, p. 243.

This type of opera is again represented by *La Corona d'Arianna* of 1726, which obviously pleased the Court so much that it was performed three times in the gardens of the 'Favorita'. The libretto was again by Pariati, who combined the love story of Ariadne and Bacchus with that of Thetis and Peleus. As in so many of his other works he uses trumpets to give the orchestration a festive character. However, the most original use of a solo trumpet is made in the aria of Bacchus, in which he declares that in future he will care less about heroic deeds than about the pursuit of love:

In the same year Fux wrote an oratorio *Il Testamento di Nostro Signor Gesù Cristo sul Calvario*, to a libretto by Pariati. It is the longest of all his oratorios, but not as good as the others, because Fux had to deal with too copious a text. Quite different is the music of his last oratorio, *La Deposizione dalla croce di Gesù Cristo Salvator nostro*, produced in 1728, the libretto for which was written by Claudio Pasquini. It was performed on 23 March in the Imperial Chapel, and the performance was repeated in 1738. Pasquini had been engaged to replace Apostolo Zeno (who wanted to return to Venice, and left Vienna in 1729,) and also to assist Pariati, whose creative powers had diminished.

However, one poet was not enough to supply the composer's demands. In 1729, therefore, Charles VI engaged as Court Poet the young Abate Pietro Metastasio, whose reputation had been rising for some time. He became the librettist of Fux's last opera, *Enea negli Elisi*, performed in the 'Favorita' Palace gardens on 28 August 1731 in the presence of the Turkish Ambassador, 'who not only enjoyed the music but was also pleased by the courteous attention which he received.'[32]

Times had changed; Turkey was no longer a threat to the Empire. Times had changed in opera, too: though *Enea negli Elisi* is still a 'festa teatrale' to celebrate the fortieth birthday of the Empress, the libretto is more lyrical in character than those of Pariati. We no longer have the High Baroque style in Metastasio's verses, but the 'stilo galante'. This master of the libretto was such a powerful personality that Madame de Staël in her *Corinne* was to compare him with Dante, Petrarch, Ariosto, Guarini, and Tasso.[33] His fame as a poet survived long after composers had given up setting his librettos to music.

Metastasio was at the beginning of his brilliant career when he wrote *Enea negli Elisi*, a somewhat superficial panegyric of the virtues of the Empress. But even here the beauty of Metastasio's lines can be felt, that rare gift which made it so easy for the composers to set his words to music. Fux treated the sinfonia as a piece of brilliant sound for four trumpets, and wrote choruses which show that he was still in full possession of his creative genius. In the arias we feel he was even more adventurous. He was beginning to develop a classical line which might have resulted in a new style, had not the death of his wife in the same year put an end to his dramatic career.

Does this mean that Fux was so affected by the loss of the woman who had been his companion for thirty-five years that he gave up composing altogether? It is possible, though there may be another explanation for the ending of his dramatic career. Fux remained almost to his death the first Conductor to the Imperial Court. Though Charles VI had a great admiration for the servant of three Emperors, he would not have been able to retain him in that highly responsible post if Fux had failed to fulfil his obligations. It is true that Fux seems to have felt he could no longer bear the strain of writing operas as well as rehearsing and conducting them, and that he left the latter tasks henceforth mainly to Antonio Caldara and Francesco Conti. But he may have concentrated again on writing music for the church; this suggestion is supported by

[32] *Wiener Diarium* of September 5 1731.
[33] S. Worsthorne, 'Metastasio and the history of Opera', in *The Cambridge Journal*, vi (1953), pp. 534–45.

the very great number of liturgical compositions which we have already mentioned. This would fit very well into the picture of a man who began as a choirboy, wrote for many years exclusively for the liturgical service and never ceased to write sacred music and oratorios. In this field he had always been an unparalleled master, undisturbed by the changes in the style of secular music. Here he was able to continue writing the music which lived in him, and to hand on his legacy to those who were to hear and sing his masses and graduals in the Imperial Chapel and St. Stephan's Cathedral long after his death.

So it was that Joseph Haydn, who came to Vienna in the year of Fux's death, grew up in the master's musical atmosphere and tradition. He sang his masses in the Cathedral, and learned to compose from the *Gradus*. The legacy which Haydn received from Fux was to be enriched by the wealth of his own genius. Seen in this light, Johann Joseph Fux appears not only as the great master of his own epoch but as the ancestor of the Viennese Classical School.